essence of WHITE

Hilary Mandleberg

essence of WHITE

William Morrow and Company, Inc.

New York

Designer   Luis Peral-Aranda
Location Research   Nadine Bazar and Kate Brunt
Production   Patricia Harrington
Head of Design   Gabriella Le Grazie
Publishing Director   Anne Ryland

Library of Congress Cataloging-in-Publication Data

Mandleberg, Hilary.
Essence of white / by Hilary Mandleberg.
p.   cm.
ISBN 0-688-17432-9
1. Color in interior decoration. 2. White. I. Title.
NK2115.5.C6M3627 2000
747' .94—dc21   99-37354
                                          CIP
Printed and bound in China by Toppan Printing Co.

First Edition
10 9 8 7 6 5 4 3 2 1
www.williammorrow.com

contents

shades & textures

If all the earth were paper white

John Lyly

Nature so rarely manages to achieve pure white. Freshly fallen snow with sunlight bouncing off it, or white clouds scudding across a clear blue sky may come close, but just see how a small hollow in the snow casts a shadow of blue, or how the thinned-out

SHADES OF WHITE

edges of the clouds are a wistful pale gray. And if you thought that a white flower was white, then look again. Bright yellow stamens pour out a rich buttermilk pool. Petals are colored shyly with a soft blush or glow gently green with the reflection of the leaves.

White is gently romantic or starkly
modern, depending on how you use it.
With sunlight filtering through, even

a heavy canvas curtain can look light
and airy, while a classic metal lamp
sheds a cool and otherworldly glow.

Does white conjure up an image of clinical cleanliness, stark utility, or just the boringly bland? It need not. Texture is the secret ingredient that brings white to life and turns it into an exciting sensory experience. The subtle interplay of light and shade as

TEXTURES

light reflects off a surface lets you distinguish between gauzy, fine white muslin, the delicately fragile petals of a simple white flower, sparkling white enameled cookware, intricate filigreed lace, freshly starched damask, or the matte density of white-painted walls.

Mix your textures to liven up white-on-white decorating schemes. Stick to natural materials, irregular surfaces,

and organic elements for a country feel, or smoothly finished manmade details for a more contemporary look.

living/dining

What could be more soothing than a living room painted in the purest of whites? An all-white backdrop will emphasize the shape and texture of objects in the room—an antique wooden bowl, a battered painted table, or a shiny leather chair. And as the day

CLASSIC WHITE

progresses and the light moves around the room, white shows itself to be infinitely complex, a far cry from monochrome. These are the subtleties that help to make it a classic. But ever since decorating first began, achieving the perfect white has been something of an obsession. People have tried anything and everything—crushed and powdered bones, pearls,

shells—but the results were dirty off-whites or whites that quickly turned yellow. Then, in the 1920s, titanium white was born. This wonder pigment is permanent, nontoxic, does not go yellow, and covers well. Soon it was

adopted by the modernists as their signature color. Now we wonder how we ever managed without pure white.

White is the classic color choice for elegant dining. It creates the relaxed mood you need for pleasant meals and shows food off to its best advantage.

DINING IN WHITE

kitchen

Working in a serene, uncluttered white kitchen will help any cook stay calm in a crisis. To create the effect of an airy sundrenched beach house kitchen, choose white walls, stripped floorboards, pale wood counter tops and a matching dining table. A lone

NOW AND ZEN

dark wood armoire, a trio of woven baskets, and a simple carved wooden bowl, together with a white orchid in a dark ceramic pot, will add just a hint of subtly restrained contrast and understated eastern elegance and will add to the deep sense of tranquility.

Gleaming white surfaces practically state "germ-free," which makes white the ideal choice for the ultimate hygienic kitchen. If your taste leans toward the austere, then you'll love the sharp, uncluttered lines of flush white doors, stainless steel and clean-cut marble. Everything in its place and a place for everything. Introduce a slightly softer but no less business-like note with wooden counter tops and the occasional wooden cabinet front, or add coziness to an all-white kitchen with a thoughtfully chosen display of utensils that bridges the gap between modern and country. And if it's nostalgia you're after, try a splashback of bevel-edged white tiles.

bedroom

All that we see or seem
Is but a dream within a dream

Edgar Allan Poe

Floaty, filmy, feminine, and fantastic! Deck out a bedroom in romantic white for a voluptuous, sensual experience. Fairy-tale beds in warmly gleaming mahogany or sinuous cast iron entice you to your nightly slumber. Pure white antique cotton sheets and soft,

DREAMING IN WHITE

down-filled pillows embrace you while you dream. Recreate a vanished world of romance and elegance with gauzy billowing curtains and closets that open to reveal a neat stack of crisply ironed and folded bedlinens. This is the stuff that dreams are made of.

Meditate on white to lift your spirits, for white is the color of peace and comfort, the color that alleviates sadness, cleanses the emotions, and works to purify the soul. Used in the bedroom, white is gently soothing and conducive to sleep. Pared-down, fuss-free white for walls and bedding is perfection for the ultimate, minimal bedroom. But take care, for white can also be cold and isolating. Add the warmth of wood or a blend of shades and textures, then feel the serenity.

Lightness and a sense of space go hand in hand with white, and this cool, somewhat oriental bedroom shows why.

Subtle light effects, minimal furniture, and an expanse of window with just a hint of a blind accentuate the mood.

bathroom

Bathtubs are frequently tucked away in the smallest, most somber room in the house. So what better way to make them feel spacious than to create an all-white bathroom around them? For long bath-time soaks, imagine sinking deep into a huge old-fashioned white-

BATHING BELLE

enameled bathtub with claw feet, then wrapping up in a soft white bathrobe. For quick cleanups, modern minimal white is the no-nonsense choice. And so minimal doesn't end up as clinical, add some natural texture—touches of wood, pumice, cork, and a real sponge.

. . . a white celestial thought

Henry Vaughan

White is famous as a symbol of purity and cleanliness; sunlight streaming through the window accentuates these

associations. It's no wonder then that pure white has always been and still continues to be a bathroom favorite.

outside

White makes a glorious choice for gardens. Scintillatingly bright in the sun, it looks great in shady corners too. Enjoy the luminous contrast of white flowers against dark foliage, particularly on summer evenings, and remember that, since white recedes,

SUN OR SHADE

white blooms at the end of the garden will make it appear longer. Clothe a garden in scented white jasmine for the ultimate night-time sensory experience or bring the Mediterranean look to even the smallest of courtyards by painting it white, right down to its flowerpots.

A cluster of limewashed houses dazzles the eye in the summer sun. In hot climates especially, limewash has been used for centuries to help keep brickwork and plaster, stables and outhouses cool and clean. It bonds with the surface to form a thin layer of lime that acts as a disinfectant. In many parts of the world, the annual visit from the itinerant lime-washer is still one of the highlights of the spring-cleaning season.

White furniture can blend effortlessly with any garden setting, traditional or contemporary. And it's so easy to

dress up inexpensive junk-shop finds to make original, funky pieces. Just rub down wood or metal, then apply one or two coats of white paint. If you're feeling adventurous, transform a white cotton roller-towel and a few

pieces of tape into a seat cover, or beautify a tired old director's chair with a loose cover made from canvas.

credits

Architects and designers whose work is featured in this book:

Key: a=above, b=below, l=left, r=right, t=telephone, f=fax

Barefoot Elegance

Dot Spikings & Jennifer Castle

Interior Designers

3537 Old Coneyo Road

Suite 105

Newbury Park

CA91320

USA

t 805 499 5959

Pages 20, 30

Alexandra Champalimaud & Associates Inc.

Interior Architecture and Design

One Union Square West

Suite 603

New York

NY 10003

USA

t 212 807 8869

f 212 807 1742

Page 52

Françoise Dorget

Interior Designer

Caravane

6 rue Pavée

75004 Paris

France

t 00 33 (0)1 44 61 04 20

f 00 33 (0)1 44 61 04 22

Pages 56, 58-59

Mark Guard Architects

161 Whitfield Street

London W1P 5RY

t 00 44 (0)20 7380 1199

Pages 44-45

Alastair Hendy

Food writer, art director and designer

f 00 44 (0)20 7739 6040

Page 29 l & r

Littman Goddard Hogarth

Architects

12 Chelsea Wharf

15 Lots Road

London

SW10 0QJ

t 00 44 (0)20 7351 7871

Pages 2, 22 **r**

Roger Oates Design

Specialist in English flatweave rugs and runners

The Long Barn

Eastnor

Ledbury

Herefordshire

HR8 1EL

t 00 44 (0)1531 632718

Pages 19 **r**, 24-25

Vicente Wolf Associates Inc.

Architects

333 West 39th Street

New York

NY 10018

USA

t 212 465 0590

Page 23 **l**

Woolf Architects

39-51 Highgate Road

London NW5 1RT

t 00 44 (0)20 7428 9500

Pages 4-5, 18, 33 main & inset **b**, 34 **al**, 43

photographers

Front cover main & inset Henry Bourne; **Back cover** James Merrell; **Spine** Henry Bourne; **Front flap** Henry Bourne;

Back flap David Loftus; **I** Henry Bourne; **2** Andrew Wood/an apartment in London designed by Littman Goddard Hogarth

Architects; **3** Pia Tryde; **4–5** Andrew Wood/David Jermyn's house in London designed by Woolf Architects; **6–7** Henry Bourne;

8 Tom Leighton; **9** David Loftus; **10 l** Ray Main; **10 r** Henry Bourne; **11** Ray Main; **12** Henry Bourne; **13** Tom Leighton;

14 David Loftus; **15 al, ar & bl** Tom Leighton; **15 br** James Merrell; **16** Tom Leighton; **17 l & r** Henry Bourne;

18 Andrew Wood/Patricia Ijaz's house in London designed by Woolf Architects; **19 l** Henry Bourne; **19 r** Tom Leighton/

Roger Oates & Fay Morgan's house in Herefordshire; **20** Simon Upton/a house designed by Barefoot Elegance;

21 Simon Upton/Ricardo Regazzoni & Guido Stockman's house in Mexico; **22 l** James Merrell/a house designed by Janie Jackson,

stylist and designer; **22 r** Andrew Wood/an apartment in London designed by Littman Goddard Hogarth Architects;

23 l James Merrell/Vicente Wolf's apartment in New York; **23 r** James Merrell/Gabriele Sanders' apartment in New York;

24–25 Tom Leighton/Roger Oates & Fay Morgan's house in Herefordshire; **26–27** Henry Bourne; **28** James Merrell;

29 l & r Andrew Wood/Alastair Hendy & John Clinch's apartment in London designed by Alastair Hendy; **30** Simon Upton/

a house designed by Barefoot Elegance; **31** Tom Leighton; **33 main & inset b** Andrew Wood/Patricia Ijaz's house in London

designed by Woolf Architects; **33 inset a** James Merrell; **34 al** Andrew Wood/David Jermyn's house in London designed by Woolf

Architects; **34 ar** James Merrell; **34 bl** Pia Tryde; **34 br** James Merrell; **35** James Merrell/Robyn & Simon Carnachan's house in

Auckland; **36** Henry Bourne; **37 l** James Merrell; **37 r** Tom Leighton; **38–39** Tom Leighton; **40 al, bl & br** Henry Bourne;

40 ar Tom Leighton; **41** James Merrell/Gabriele Sanders' apartment in New York; **42** James Merrell/a house in London designed

by Janie Jackson, stylist and designer; **43** Andrew Wood/Patricia Ijaz's house in London designed by Woolf Architects;

44–45 Ray Main/a house in London designed by Mark Guard Architects; **46** James Merrell; **47 l** Henry Bourne;

47 r Andrew Wood; **48** David Montgomery; **49** Henry Bourne; **50–51** Andrew Wood; **52** Simon Upton/a house in Connecticut

designed by Alexandra Champalimaud & Associates Inc; **53 l & r** David Montgomery; **54–55** Pia Tryde; **56** Simon Upton;

57 Pia Tryde; **58–59** Simon Upton; **60 l** Henry Bourne; **60 r** Pia Tryde; **61 l & r** Pia Tryde; **62–63** Pia Tryde; **64** Pia Tryde;

Endpapers Henry Bourne